# Clean Eating

Fire up Your Weight Loss and Energy with Delicious Clean Eating Recipes

**Cathy Harwell**

Cathy Harwell

© **Copyright 2016 by Pinnacle Publishers, LLC - All rights reserved.**

This document is geared towards providing exact and reliable information in regards to the topic and issue covered. The publication is sold with the idea that the publisher is not required to render accounting, officially permitted, or otherwise, qualified services. If advice is necessary, legal or professional, a practiced individual in the profession should be ordered.

- From a Declaration of Principles which was accepted and approved equally by a Committee of the American Bar Association and a Committee of Publishers and Associations.

In no way is it legal to reproduce, duplicate, or transmit any part of this document in either electronic means or in printed format. Recording of this publication is strictly prohibited and any storage of this document is not allowed unless with written permission from the publisher. All rights reserved.

The information provided herein is stated to be truthful and consistent, in that any liability, in terms of inattention or otherwise, by any usage or abuse of any policies, processes, or directions contained within is the solitary and utter responsibility of the recipient reader. Under no circumstances will any legal responsibility or blame be held against the publisher for any reparation, damages, or monetary loss due to the information herein, either directly or indirectly.

Respective authors own all copyrights not held by the publisher.

*Clean Eating*

The information herein is offered for informational purposes solely, and is universal as so. The presentation of the information is without contract or any type of guarantee assurance.

The trademarks that are used are without any consent, and the publication of the trademark is without permission or backing by the trademark owner. All trademarks and brands within this book are for clarifying purposes only and are the owned by the owners themselves, not affiliated with this document.

# Contents

| | |
|---|---|
| Introduction | v |
| Chapter 1: What Is Clean Eating | 1 |
| Chapter 2: How to Get Started | 6 |
| Chapter 3: Let's Start Eating Right -The first three weeks | 13 |
| Chapter 4: Three Week Diet Plan | 29 |
| Chapter 5 : Snacks and Deserts | 32 |
| Chapter 6: Clean Eating Tips | 35 |
| Conclusion | 38 |
| Related Reading | 39 |
| Stop… Before you close this book get your free bonus… | 41 |
| Check Out My Other Books | 45 |

# Introduction

I want to thank you and congratulate you for buying the book, "Clean Eating Diet – Fire up Your Weight Loss and Energy with Delicious Clean Eating Recipes".

This book contains everything you need to know about eating clean and healthy. Eating healthy food has become a difficult thing to accomplish in today's world. Unknown to most people 80% of the food in grocery stores in America contain added sugar, and many of them have processed additives with unnatural chemicals as well. These can wreak havoc on your body, making it impossible to lose weight and enjoy a fit healthy body. Fortunately, there is a way to combat all of these "additives" and that is by eating clean. By using the recipes in this book you will be able to live a healthier life all while losing weight faster than ever before!

Thanks again for buying this book, I hope you enjoy it!

# Chapter 1: What Is Clean Eating

From the internet to recipe books to documentaries, clean eating is taking the United States by storm. It seems that everywhere we look, there is something being mentioned about clean eating and even when we are talking to our friends we find out that they are getting on the bandwagon.

So what exactly is clean eating and why is it being accepted by so many people all of a sudden. Clean eating is actually a very simple lifestyle that involves eating only whole foods. In other words, it removes all of the processed foods out of one's diet and replaces those foods with foods that are natural.

Before we go further I want to make sure that you understand that this is not some type of fad diet. Instead, this is a lifestyle change where you are eating the foods that your body was actually made to eat.

Before you decide to take part in this lifestyle change and before we learn exactly what clean eating is, we need to understand why it is important. Let's first take a look at processed foods.

## *What are processed foods and what are they doing to your body?*

Processed foods are any food that is not in its natural form or contains more than 3 ingredients (you must know what these ingredients are in order for it not to be processed). One example of a food that has more than one ingredient that is not considered processed is butter. The ingredients in butter are cream and salt. This is not considered a processed food when it comes to clean eating.

On the other hand vegetable oil spreads contain many ingredients and most of them you cannot pronounce and chances are that you have no idea what they are.

In other words, processed foods are any food that is made in a lab by men that are in lab coats. <u>Processed food is going to make you fat and sick.</u> Studies have shown that since your body does not know how to process these foods, it turns the food into fat instead of energy.

This brings us to the diet and exercise revolution. Back in the 50's it was considered taboo for people to exercise. Then one doctor decided that if people wanted to lose weight they needed to exercise more. This was because he had been watching mice, the heavier mice ate the same amount of food as the thinner mice, but the doctor observed that the larger mice were less active after they ate.

This was when everyone decided that all you needed to do was eat less and exercise more. The problem with that is that since this exercise revolution, more and more people are obese. The fact is that right now, 2 out of every 3 people are considered overweight. How can this be when everyone is eating reduced fat, low fat, added fiber diet foods?

It is because of the food that is being put into our bodies. This is not to say that exercise is not needed to be healthy but what I am saying is that we are not going to exercise our way thin. So if we are not going to be able to exercise ourselves thin that leaves us to look at calories.

We all know that no matter how we burn a calorie, whether it be when we are exercising or when we are asleep it is still a calorie burned, but the question is: Is a calorie eaten still a calorie eaten?

## Clean Eating

The answer is a resounding NO. In order to understand this, let's look at 160 calories worth of almonds. When we eat the almonds it takes our body longer to digest them because of the fiber. This means that our blood sugar levels rise and stay fairly steady for the entire amount of time that our body is digesting the almonds.

What if we drink 160 calories worth of soda? The sugar gets absorbed straight into the liver, giving the liver a 'sugar rush' which causes our blood sugar to spike. When your liver gets that amount of sugar, it has no other choice but to start turning it into fat.

This means that if you eat 160 calories in almonds you are going to be fueling your body, whereas if you drink 160 calories of soda you are going to be adding fat to your body.

Another problem that we face is that we are being shown a message that does not back up the science. How many commercials do you see on television where a thin person is drinking a soda and they are so happy? You never see an obese person drinking soda because companies know that this would not sell.

Think about when cigarettes were not seen as a health risk. There were commercials with doctors smoking them, everyone that smoked them looked happy and healthy and not one was coughing their lungs out. Today we know that cigarettes are very bad for us.

In much the same way we see all of these commercials on television telling us that processed food is going to make us feel awesome and it is so healthy because it is reduced fat, but we are beginning to understand that just like the big tobacco companies lied to us, food companies are lying to us as well.

## *What is the proof?*

The fact is that processed foods are full of refined sugar. Studies have shown that refined sugar is nothing more than a drug to our brains and our bodies. When heroin addicted rats were given the choice between heroin water and sugar water in a recent study that was conducted, the addicted rats' choice the sugar water.

The reason behind this was that the sugar caused the same reactions in the brain as the heroin did.

Now you may be thinking that the food you buy does not contain all of this sugar because it is low fat or reduced fat or fat free but guess what? A tablespoon of sugar is fat free, a bag of sugar is fat free. Sugar is fat free but it is in no way calorie free.

When foods are processed, they become stripped of any nutrients that were in them and become flavorless. In order to bring back some of the flavor sugar is added. This same sugar causes you to become addicted just like heroin would. Do not think that the no calorie choices are any better because the sugar is simply replaced with chemicals such as aspartame or other poisonous chemicals.

Remember this, just as cigarettes cause cancer, specific foods do make you fat.

## *What is the answer?*

The only answer is to begin eating the food that our bodies were created to eat. Those foods being in their natural state or as close to their natural state as possible. This does not mean that you cannot cook your foods, but you do need to remember if you eat fruits and vegetables in their natural state you are going to absorb more vitamins.

## What about the price?

One thing that many people say is that it is less expensive to eat processed foods than it is to eat whole foods. We are going to go over several low cost meals later on in the book, but you will learn that you have been conditioned to believe this. The way this has been done is that we are bombarded with 'value' meal options, commercials saying that it is actually cheaper or more convenient for you to purchase this food.

The truth is that where it would cost about 30 dollars to feed a family of 5 at Mc Donald's, you can purchase whole foods for about 13 dollars and feed the same number of people healthier foods. That means for less than half of the price you can feed your family a healthy meal.

## Why Clean Eating?

The truth is that it does not matter what your health goal is you cannot accomplish it without clean eating. If you want to reduce your risk of heart disease you can only do so with clean eating. If you want to lose weight you can only do so with clean eating (if you want to keep it off long term).

One of the great benefits of clean eating is that it helps to remove all of the chemicals and toxins out of your body. It is about getting back to basics about eating the foods that your body was designed to eat and eliminating the foods that your body is unable to process.

Finally, it is about giving your body the nourishment that it needs and is craving so badly. It is about taking care of you.

# Chapter 2: How to Get Started

Now that you understand why it is important to eat clean and what clean eating really is you may be wondering what you need to do in order to get started. Some people will tell you that you need to go into your kitchen right now and get rid of all of the processed foods. While I do think that it is important for you to get the processed foods out of your home, I am not going to tell you to do this.

What I am going to tell you is that you need to make a decision. Your choice right now is to begin to reduce the amount of processed foods that you consume and replace these with whole foods or you can eliminate all of the processed foods and completely replace them with whole foods.

It is possible for you to be successful when you eliminate all of the processed foods all at once, but you need to understand that you are going to deal with cravings and sugar withdrawals. These withdrawals and cravings can last up to a week and each time that you give in to the cravings you will have to start over so they can last a long time.

Personally, I think that you will be more successful if you eliminate all of the processed food at one time but it is a very personal decision. Of course, this does not mean that you will never get to go out to dinner with your friends to eat or you will never get to have a slice of cake again. What this does mean is that you can on occasion eat some of this food, but the key word is occasionally. This does not mean daily or even weekly.

The next thing that you need to think about is what you are drinking. So many times we are filling ourselves full of fizzy drinks in order to quench our thirst, but we are doing ourselves a disservice.

You need to start focusing on the amount of water that you are drinking. As I stated earlier in this book clean eating is going to help to eliminate the toxins in your body and one way to help speed this process up is to drink a lot of water.

Water naturally helps to flush out all of the chemicals and toxins from our bodies and it helps to eliminate fat while boosting our metabolism. Water will also help you when it comes to the cravings that will come when you eliminate processed foods from your diet.

(1) You will need to start your day off with a glass of water instead of a cup of coffee. In the water you can squeeze the juice of one lemon for flavor and to help improve the detoxifying effects. Drink this before each meal, with each snack and before you go to bed at night. When you first begin doing this you may gain a little bit of weight, but it is water weight and as your body gets used to being hydrated once again you will see the weight melting off of you.

Now we need to think about what foods we can eat. Fresh fruits and vegetables are going to be the main part of your diet when it comes to clean eating. If it grows on a tree or out of the ground you will be able to eat it in abundance. You can have as much fruit as you want because unlike refined sugar, the sugar in fruit is actually good for you and your body knows how to process it. This means that you are not going to be experiencing spikes in your blood sugar levels like you would if you were eating a candy bar or a bag of potato chips.

Fresh fruit and vegetables make great snacks throughout the day and you can even create healthy smoothies from them. You do need to avoid all processed fruit juice and  vegetable juice. The reason for this is 1. It is processed so

*No Processed Fruit Juice*

there are going to be a ton of extra chemicals and other ingredients added, 2. All of the fiber has been taken out of the fruits and vegetables and all you are left with is the sugar. This means that instead of having a stable blood sugar level <u>your blood sugar levels will spike just as they would if you were eating a candy bar.</u>

Meat is the next thing that I want to talk about. Some people are going to tell you that you need to eat lean meats because the fatty meats will cause you to gain weight. I am going to tell you to <u>eat the fatty meats.</u> The reason for this is that our bodies need a certain amount of fat in order to function properly. These need to be healthy fats that come from natural sources. Of course you can eat vegetables such as <u>avocados</u> to get some of these fats, but you need to <u>make sure that you are getting it from your meat</u> as well. You do not have to avoid bacon or other fatty cuts because this is what your body needs to function properly.

If we do not eat these healthy fats our brains will slow down and become foggy, our bodies will become exhausted and we will lack motivation and we will start craving fats. Of course we are not going to crave healthy fats because that is not what we are used to eating. Instead, we are going to have to deal with cravings for more processed foods because our body is trying to get what it needs from what it already knows.

Dairy is another food group where people tend to get confused. We are told that we need to eat low fat vegetable oil spread, low fat milk, low fat cheeses, low fat yogurt and low fat everything. <u>The truth is that you need to eat full fat when it comes to dairy</u> products. The reason for this is the same as why you want to eat fatty meats. Our bodies need the fat that comes with these products. Consuming fat does not make you fat. We have already learned that what is making people fat is the over consumption of refined sugars that are found in processed foods. Fat allows our bodies to function properly and burn more calories.

I want to talk for a minute about vegetable oil spreads. This was created by farmers to help fatten their cattle, but it was found that instead it made their cattle sick. Not wanting to lose all of the money that they invested in the creation of the product they added some food coloring, a bit of flavoring and marketed it as a healthy substitute for butter. It is important to note that these spreads only have one ingredient different than plastic and contain 27 of the same ingredients as paint.

When you buy a tub of this spread you can actually take it outside, open it up and no bugs, no flies, and nothing will touch it because even the bugs realize it is not food. No bacteria will even grow in it. This is not food. You need to instead choose real butter that is made from cream and has no chemicals in it. Remember, choose the foods that are as close to their natural state as possible. Skim milk is not the closest we can come to the natural state of milk.

Grains are important as well. This is one area that so many people tend to overlook, but we need to remember that our bodies need more grains than any other food group if we want them to function properly. What we have to avoid is bleached enriched grains. White grains, white flour, white rice have all been stripped of their vitamins during the bleaching process and then have been enriched with artificial vitamins, which of course are not nearly as good as the natural nutrients.

Instead, focus on whole grains, oats, brown rice, quinoa and whole wheat pasta. Remember to look for brown grains. This means that they have not been processed to the extent of white grains. Many of them such as steel cut oats have not been processed at all. Whole wheat pasta is on the fence, but if you desire pasta without having to make it yourself which is a long process it is okay to have on occasion.

That is what you are going to eat from now on. If you want ice cream, you are going to have to <u>learn how to make it yourself from your own whole ingredien</u>ts. You are going to have to spend some time in the kitchen and if you do not know how to cook, this can be frustrating at first, but the recipes that I am going to give you are going to walk you through the process and make it very easy for you to do.

I do want to note that if you are a very busy person like I am you might want to consider using freezer meals. This way you will have everything that you need ready to go for each day and you don't have to worry about being tempted to run out and grab a pizza because it really is easier to grab your pre-prepped meal and either place it in the crock pot or on the stove. This will take several hours to prepare, but it is possible. Personally, I set back one day a month to go grocery shopping and to do all of the prepping. Then I allow a certain amount of money each week for fresh fruits, veggies, milk and butter as needed. This has actually reduced my grocery bill by 75 percent so that is another benefit. This of course is just something for you to think about and I am not going to go into depth about it in this book but wanted to give you an idea about how you can work this plan into a busy lifestyle.

## *You have to make a plan.*

I am hoping that this book will help you to create a plan of your own because without a plan you are not going to succeed at clean eating. I know that sometimes we all like to go to the store, grab a bunch of stuff that looks good and decide that we will come up with meals on the fly but you cannot do that with clean eating.

## Clean Eating

The reason is 1. You will go broke and 2. You will not come up with any meals, the food will rot in your fridge and you will find yourself grabbing pizza or drive thru food on the way home from work.

Planning is key. You need to know exactly what you will eat for breakfast, lunch and dinner every single day. You need to know what your snacks will be and where they are. This will help you from becoming tempted to grab quick foods out of vending machines or from fast food restaurants.

You also need to know what you are going to do if the craving hits you. One great thing that I found was at a store I frequent. The chocolate oranges were made of dark chocolate and only contained three ingredients and I knew what the ingredients were. I was also able to find cocoa coated honey candy that only contained 2 ingredients. These were my go to during the first few weeks when my body felt like it was going to die if I did not have any sugar.

The great thing about this was that there was no sugar in them, but just the sweet taste has been enough to trick my body into thinking it had gotten what it wanted and calmed the cravings.

Remember that eating clean does not mean that you are never going to get to eat treats again. In fact it means quite the opposite. Later in the book I am going to give you great recipes that you can use to create healthy, tasty treats, even cookies are not off limits. It just comes down to what you are putting in the cookies.

The great thing about clean eating is that you never have to feel deprived. You don't have to consume yourself with the idea of calories in versus calories burned. You don't have to limit your portions and get up from the table feeling as if you are starving. You actually get to eat more meals than you were before.

This brings me to the idea of eating 5 small meals per day. When I talk about small meals I am not talking about a banana as a meal. I am talking about a meal that consists of protein, grain, fruit, vegetable, healthy fats and carbohydrates.

Your original three meals will be slightly larger than the other two, but think of it like this. Instead of eating three meals that fill a regular dinner plate you want to eat 5 meals that fill a salad plate. By using a salad plate not only will you reduce your portion sizes, but you will trick your brain into thinking you ate more than you actually did.

You will not be hungry because you will be eating foods that are full of fiber and take longer to digest and will be eating more often ensuring that your blood sugar levels do not drop. This will keep your metabolism at a steady level throughout the day and will help you to have more energy and burn more calories.

# Chapter 3: Let's Start Eating Right -The first three weeks

Now that you understand how important it is for you to focus on clean eating instead of dieting in order to lose weight or reach your health goals you may be wondering exactly what you are going to eat. I mean, let's face it, a handful of carrots with a side of baked chicken breast and an apple just doesn't sound that appetizing does it?

In this chapter I want to go over 3 weeks' worth of meals that you can use while making the clean eating change in your life. I will give you breakfasts, lunches, dinners and even snacks and desserts that will help you not only lose weight but detoxify your body and become healthier.

## *Week 1 – Breakfast*
### Overnight oatmeal-

This should be your go to breakfast most mornings when you are clean eating. I am going to give you other breakfast ideas for when you are in a hurry or maybe you forget to put your oatmeal on but this one is going to give you everything you need to start your morning out right.

For this recipe you will need steel cut oats. I do not recommend making this recipe with any other type of oat because of the long cooking time.

- ½ cup oats
- 2 cup water
- ½ tsp. Cinnamon
- 1 tsp. Vanilla

- ½ cup dried cranberries or raisins
- Maple syrup

This recipe is for a small 1 or 2 quart crock pot so if you are using a larger crock pot you will want to increase the size of the recipe. First, you will need to mix your oats, water, vanilla and cinnamon into your slow cooker. You can also add the raisins or cranberries at this time if you don't mind that they are soft when you eat them. If you want them chewy you can add them when you are ready to serve the oats, but will want to use some honey to sweeten it. You need to cook this on low for about 8 hours and top with maple syrup before serving. Since you are focusing on clean eating you need to make sure that you are using pure maple syrup. Of course, there are many different ways for you to prepare your overnight oats if this specific recipe does not sound good to you. You may choose strawberry banana or another flavor, but you will still follow a basic recipe of ½ a cup of steel cut oats to 2 cups of water and then the rest of your ingredients.

**Protein packed pancakes** - This is a great weekend breakfast that you can have with the family and even though it seems like they are getting a treat they are eating a nice healthy clean breakfast.

This recipe will make about 7 pancakes-

You will need:

- 12 eggs
- 1 cup of quick oats
- Olive oil spray (to coat the pan)
- 1 tsp of cinnamon

- Maple syrup
- A nonstick pan

The first thing that you want to do is mix the eggs, oats and cinnamon in a bowl. Then spray your non-stick pan with olive oil. Place your pancakes into the pan and cook just like a regular pancake. Each pancake is about 1 ladle full of the mix, but depending on the size of your ladle you should get around 6-8 pancakes out of this recipe.

You can add any clean topping that you like strawberries, bananas, syrup or whatever you choose. Some people simply place butter on them and eat them as they head out the door. It is completely up to you.

This is a great recipe if you are wanting you use freezer meals, but you should know that it is not one of the cheaper meals and I would personally only serve it on the weekends due to the rising price of eggs.

**Oatmeal muffins**

I hope that you are seeing a trend here when it comes to breakfast. I cannot stress how important it is for you to use oatmeal in your breakfast to ensure that you are getting enough grains.

For this recipe you will need-

- 3 cups of oatmeal
- 1 cup of milk
- 1 tbsp. Baking powder
- 1 tbsp. Cinnamon
- 4 very ripe bananas

- 2 eggs

- 1 tsp. Vanilla extract

You can also add in blueberries, diced apples, chopped strawberries or even nuts. A few tablespoons of protein powder will help make this a nice protein packed breakfast as well.

This can be a make ahead breakfast so that all you need to do is grab your muffin and go each morning.

Each muffin is going to contain 69 calories, 1.4 grams of fat, 12 grams of carbs, 2 grams of fiber and 2.5 grams of protein. This means that you can grab a few muffins as you head out the door, sit down to a meal and have the muffin as a side or even enjoy them as a snack throughout your day.

Smash the ripe bananas into a mixing bowl with a fork until the lumps are gone add the oatmeal, milk, baking powder, cinnamon, eggs and vanilla extract mixing well. Line your muffin tin with paper liners and fill them with the batter. These muffins will not rise high, so do not worry about over filling. Bake the muffins at 375 for 20 minutes, then let cool for about 10 minutes. You will want to store these in a zip lock bag if you are not eating them right away.

These can be frozen and laid out the night before you plan on eating them or kept in the refrigerator for up to three days. When it comes to freezing breakfast foods I suggest that you keep it to a minimum, especially if you do not have a large freezer chest.

**Bacon and Eggs**

Of course, this had to make the cut. It is an all American breakfast one that many people have begun to avoid, but no longer have to. Prepare your eggs however you prefer. Bacon cooks the best in the oven on a cookie sheet. Save your left over bacon fat for cooking later. Remember, it is important to get fat into your diet. This is one way that you can insure you are getting the fat needed. You can add in some whole grain clean eating approved toast with a bit of butter and you have yourself an amazing breakfast.

Now, as you can see I have only included 3 regular breakfasts and 1 weekend breakfast. The reason for this is because when you first start clean eating you want to keep things as simple as possible. I suggest that you choose one breakfast per week and eat that every day for that entire week. Not only will this make things easier on you, but it will also cut down on the price of food because you will be getting fewer ingredients

## *Lunches*

For lunches most of the time I recommend that you increase your dinner portions so that you are able to have some for lunch the following day, but of course this is not always possible and you will have to learn what portions you will need when you are first starting out. One thing that I have found is that when people are first starting out with clean eating they tend to think they will eat less than they really will. For that reason I suggest that you allow an extra ½ portion per meal per person when you are creating your meals. If you do not eat all of the food it can be used in a future meal, but having extra is always better than not having enough.

**Tuna in lettuce wraps**

Personally, I try to avoid as much bread as possible, choosing to get my grains from other sources. Because of this I choose to use other options when it comes to bread.

You will need:

- Lettuce
- Tomato
- Avocado
- Tuna packed in water
- Chopped onions
- Celery
- 1 tbsp. Lemon juice

Chop the avocado, onions, tomato and celery. Mix with the tuna and lemon juice. Place the mixture into lettuce leaves and serve. This is great with cottage cheese and a piece of your favorite fruit.

**Rice bowl**

Sometimes there is nothing better than a nice rice bowl, but rice alone is not going to give you the nutrients that you need. So for a healthy dinner that is going to give you the vitamins that you need to give you the energy you desire try this rice bowl.

You will need:

- ½ cup Brown rice cooked
- ½ avocado, chopped
- ½ of a tomato chopped
- Low sodium organic soy sauce to taste
- Salt and pepper
- Sesame seeds if desired

In a small bowl, mix the precooked rice, tomato and soy sauce. Add in salt and pepper as well as sesame seeds. You can also add in any veggies that you happen to have on hand as well if you like. Crushed red pepper flakes can be used to spice it up if you desire that extra kick as well.

## Banana Wrap

As I have said I do not like to eat bread too often, but I love using whole wheat wraps in my meals instead. This is a great lunch for anyone who is eating clean and it is very healthy. This can also be used as a snack too.

You will need:

- 1 whole wheat tortilla
- ¼ cup of clean eating approved peanut butter or other nut butter
- 1 banana
- You can also add Chia seeds, flax seed, strawberries or any other ingredient of your choice.

Place your tortilla on a flat surface and spread the peanut butter or other nut butter over the shell, you will want to stay near the center but try to spread it as thin as you can. Place your banana in the center of the tortilla shell, then roll your shell around your banana. Slice this in half.

## Pizza-DIA

This is a great weekend lunch that the kids will even love. It is packed full of all of the nutrients that your body needs and eliminates the need for packaged pizzas.

You will need:

- All of your favorite pizza toppings (that are clean)

- Cheese
- Sauce to put on your pizza (clean)
- Whole wheat tortilla shells

To make these you have two choices. The first one you can make on top of the stove. Place your tortilla shell on a flat surface spreading the sauce on one half. Add your toppings followed by your cheese and fold the other half of the shell over on top of the cheese. Spray your pan with olive oil and cook on medium until the cheese is melted and shell is slightly crunchy.

The second option is to simply make mini pizzas out of the ingredients. In order to do this, you need to place your shells on a flat surface, spread sauce over the shell, add your toppings, and then add your cheese. Cook this in the oven at 350 until cheese is melted. (This is a huge hit with kids)

## Chicken noodle soup

Of course I love to have a huge pot of chicken noodle soup made up each week for those days when I am just too busy to make anything else. This is a really great lunch for those colder months and even makes a great dinner.

You will need:

- Whole wheat pasta or brown rice
- Clean chicken broth (4 cans)
- Carrots 10 baby carrots, chopped (or 1 can of carrots)
- Celery 4 stalks, chopped.

- Precooked shredded chicken
- 1 white onion, diced

You will add all of the ingredients into a crockpot and cook on low for about 4 hours. In a separate pot you will cook your pasta or brown rice. When you are ready to eat the soup place pasta in a bowl and cover with soup. This is a great recipe to keep in the fridge, pack for work lunches and is a great go to when you are feeling sick.

Again, I have only given you 5 lunch recipes because it is best if you choose a lunch and have it every day for one week and then you can change things up the following week. You may also decide to make a few of these recipes in bulk ahead of time, place them in zip lock bags and freeze them. This will save you on prep time and will ensure that you are not getting bored with the food that you are eating each day.

## *Dinners*

Personally, I prefer to have 7 meals 4 times a month so that I am not always learning new recipes. This also helps me to ensure that the food that I am making is something that my family will eat so instead of giving you 21 dinners I am going to give you 7. If you find that one of these is not something that your family enjoys feel free to swap it out with another meal, but each of these recipes has been tested and is kid approved.

### Chili

For those times when it is getting colder outside, this has become one of the meals that my family looks forward to each week. We are not the type of family that loves beans or loves chili for that matter, but this recipe was a hit and the kids look forward to it all week long.

## Cathy Harwell

You will need-

- 1 tbsp. Olive oil
- 2 pounds ground beef
- 1 red onion, diced
- 4 cloves garlic, minced
- 2 (15 oz.) cans of dark red kidney beans
- 2 (15 oz.) cans of tomato sauce (Clean. Must have less than 3 ingredients and you must know what they are.
- 2 (14 oz.) cans of clean, diced tomatoes
- 1 (15 oz.) can of light red kidney beans
- 1 (4 oz.) can of chopped green chilies
- 1 cup of beef broth
- 2 tbsp. Chili powder
- 1 tbsp. Cumin
- 1 tsp. Salt
- ½ tsp. Black pepper.

In a large pan over medium heat you will want to heat your oil. Then add the ground beef, garlic and onions. Cook this until the beef is brown making sure that you crumble the beef as it is cooking. Drain off about ½ of the excess fat. Place the beef in the bottom of your slow cooker, add in the remaining ingredients, stirring to ensure they are combined well. Cook on low for up to 8 hours. Serve with cheese, sour cream or other topping of your choice.

When you are getting all of your ingredients, you want to make sure that they all qualify as clean ingredients. You do not want to get a ton of processed ingredients because your chili will not be any healthier than the stuff you buy in a can at the store. You can add extra spices depending on your own personal taste, but this is a good recipe to start with. You can also make this meal ahead of time in a large batch and place it in the freezer for future use.

**Beef stew**

We love the fact that many clean, dinners can be made in the crockpot without a lot of prep time and even though many people save beef stew for the winter time we love to eat it year round.

You will need:

- 2 tbsp. Olive oil
- 1 ½ lb. Beef stew meat, chopped or cubed
- 2 potatoes, cubed (you can peel or not it is up to you, we prefer to not peel)
- 10-12 baby carrots, chopped
- 1 onion, chopped into large chunks
- ½ tsp. Pepper
- 2 tbsp. Salt
- 4 cups beef stock
- 1 tbsp. Thyme, chopped
- 2 tbsp. Water.

In a large pan, heat your oil on medium heat. Place the beef stew meat into the pan and brown on all sides. Once the meat is brown, place it into the slow cooker. Top with all other ingredients, cooking on low for 8 hours. For thicker broth whisk together ¼ cup of starch with water and pour into the stew mixing as you pour. Make sure the mixture is well distributed and continue to cook for 30 more minutes. Salt if needed.

Taco Soup

You will need:

- 1 pound of ground beef
- 1 onion, chopped
- 1 pack taco seasoning
- 1 bag 16 oz. Frozen corn
- 1 16 oz. Can black beans
- 28 oz. Stewed tomatoes
- 8 oz. Tomato sauce
- 4 oz. Green chilies

Begin by browning the meat in a pan over medium heat with the onions. Once the meat is brown and the onions are cooked, drain and then place the mixture into a crock pot. Add the rest of the ingredients to the crockpot and cook on low for 4 hours. You can serve this with cheese, sour cream and tortilla shells for dipping. You may also choose to add in a bit of salsa if desired.

**Meatloaf dinner**

## Clean Eating

Yes, you can even have your southern favorites when you are practicing clean eating.

You will need:

- 3 pounds ground turkey or beef
- 1 cup whole wheat flour
- 3 eggs
- 1 onion, chopped
- 1 clove of garlic, minced
- 1 tbsp. Mustard
- 1 tbsp. Chili powder
- 1 ½ tbsp. Garlic salt
- 3 tbsp. Tomato paste
- ¼ cup milk
- 2 tbsp. Olive oil
- 1 green pepper chopped

To begin you will preheat your oven to 350 degrees and line your pan with aluminum foil. In a skillet, heat your oil and cook your onions for about 10 minutes until they are almost caramelized. Add in the garlic and turn the heat off. Leave this sitting on the burner for about 2 minutes, allowing the garlic to begin cooking.

Place all of the ingredients into a large bowl and use your hands to mix everything together, making sure that you do not burn your hands on the onions. Once everything is combined well, you will form two loaves and place them onto your already prepped pan. Cook for about 45 minutes. You can also place salsa on the top of your meatloaf. If you are used to using ketchup this is a great healthy replacement just make sure that it is clean salsa with no added sugar.

While you are cooking your meat loaf you can begin boiling corn on the cob or heating corn on top of the stove. Homemade mashed potatoes made with real butter and full fat milk are a great side to this meal as well. This is a great weekend dinner that feels like you are being bad, but in reality you are being very good.

**Beef Stir Fry**

Another one of our favorite meals beef stir fry provides all of the nutrients that you need packed full of flavor in one dish.

You will need:

- 1 cup Quinoa
- 1 tbsp. Olive oil
- 1 cup Onion, chopped
- 3 cloves of garlic, minced
- 1 yellow bell pepper, chopped
- 1 orange bell pepper, chopped
- 1 green bell pepper, chopped
- 1 cup of roasted red pepper, chopped
- 1 pound stir fry meat or beef tenderloin, cut into thin strips

- 1 cup beef broth
- ¼ cup of basil, chopped
- Salt and pepper to taste

To begin you will cook the quinoa as directed on the package, then set it aside. In a large skillet or wok, heat your olive oil on medium heat and add in your onions and garlic. Cook this until the onions are soft or about 3 minutes. Add in the green, yellow, orange and red peppers cooking for 2 more minutes. Next, you will add in the beef and cook for 2 more minutes while stirring frequently. Add in your beef broth and simmer for about 2 minutes or until the steak is cooked thoroughly. Do not turn down the heat. Once the beef has been cooked completely remove the stir fry from the heat, add in the basil, season with salt and pepper then serve over quinoa.

If you would like something besides red meat, feel free to replace the steak with shrimp or chicken.

## Chicken Fajitas

You will need-

- 1 pound cooked chicken breast, shredded
- 1 avocado, chopped
- 1 tomato, diced
- 1 cup of onion, diced
- 2 cups of mushrooms, chopped
- 1 green bell pepper, chopped
- 1 red bell pepper, chopped

- Whole wheat tortilla shells
- Cheese
- Sour cream if desired

The first thing that you want to do when you making clean chicken fajitas is to cook the chicken and shred it. In a large skillet you will add the onions to the chicken and cook them until they are almost caramelized. Add in the rest of the ingredients, cooking them until soft. Place a scoop of the mixture on your whole wheat tortilla shell, top with cheese and sour cream if desired.

That really is all that you need to follow the clean eating lifestyle for 21 days. You may be thinking that you are going to get bored with the meals, but the great thing about eating this way is that the foods are packed full of flavor and you don't get bored with them like you would bland processed food.

# Chapter 4: Three Week Diet Plan

Now that you know what you can eat over the next three weeks I want to show you how you can have variety in your diet. This is as simple as any meal plan can get and it will give your body the nutrients that it needs. Not only will your body be getting the nutrients that it need but if you follow this meal plan for 3 weeks you will begin seeing huge results.

The results that you will see is weight loss, more energy, a clearer mind, and healthier looking skin just to mention a few. Eating clean is going to affect every part of your body.

## *Week 1*
Breakfast:

- Overnight oat meal during the week
- Protein packed pancakes on the weekend

Lunch:

- Tuna, lettuce wraps during the week.
- Pizza-dia on the weekends.

Dinners- You will eat all 7 of the dinners that have been provided for you in this book. 1 each night of the week.

## *Week 2*
Breakfast:

- Oatmeal muffins during the week.
- Protein packed pancakes on the weekend.

Lunch:

- Chicken noodle soup during the week.
- Pizza Dia on the weekends

Dinners- You will eat all 7 of the dinners that have been provided for you in this book. 1 each night of the week.

# *Week 3-*

Breakfast:

- Overnight oat meal during the week.
- Eggs and Bacon on the weekend.

Lunch:

- Rice bowl during the week.
- Pizza-dia on the weekend.

Dinners - You will eat all 7 of the dinners that have been provided for you in this book. 1 each night of the week.

While you are going through your first 21 days of this lifestyle change, it is important to keep things as simple as possible. For that reason I have kept the meal plan as simple as possible. Of course it is up to you to follow the meal plan or to come up with meal ideas of your own. If you do decide to come up with meal ideas of your own you need to consider how much cooking experience you have and how much time you are wanting to put into cooking.

If you follow the plan that I have given you, you will see results by the end of the first 21 days if not sooner. The great thing about this plan is that you also get to add in two snacks and a desert!

*Clean Eating*

Of course you can choose to have a piece of fruit for your snack but I don't want to feel like I am on a diet and having fruit as a snack day end and day always makes me feel this way.

In the next chapter I am going to go over some wonderful snacks and deserts that you can have while you are following the clean eating lifestyle. You can have 2 of these snacks and 1 dessert every single day. You do not have to feel as if you cannot have any of the good treats in life because you can.

# Chapter 5 : Snacks and Deserts

One of the main reasons that many people give up on diets is because they feel so deprived. Even from day one they focus on what they cannot have but the wonderful thing about clean eating is that you don't find yourself doing that because you know you can eat snacks and deserts just like everyone else.

## *Snacks*
### Healthy Cookies

This is one of my kid's favorite snacks as well as mine and the great thing is that it only contains two amazingly healthy ingredients!

You will need:

- 2 Very ripe bananas
- 1 cup of uncooked quick oats
- ¼ cup of crushed walnuts if desired

To make these cookies you will want to begin by preheating your oven to 350 degrees, then spray your cookie sheet with cooking spray. In a bowl, mash your bananas until there are no chunks left add in the oats and walnuts folding until it is completely mixed. Place one tablespoon at a time onto cookie sheet and cook for 15 minutes. This recipe makes 16 cookies.

These cookies can be eaten for breakfast, snacks, lunch or during any other part of the day. They are very healthy and super tasty.

### Apple's and Honey

This is a very simple snack that is great when you are in a hurry or when you just need something to calm your sweet tooth. You need to make sure that you are using 100 percent real honey.

All you have to do is simply slice the apples, drizzle in honey and sprinkle with walnuts. Add a bit of cottage cheese on the side and you have a perfect mini meal.

Other snacks include: Nuts, trail mix, fruit, veggies, salads, left overs, boiled eggs, yogurt and cheeses

## *Deserts*

Frozen fruit smoothies are an item that many people run to when it comes to breakfast, but they are a great desert in place of ice cream. All you need is a bag of your favorite frozen fruit a cup of water or the juice of an orange, blend until smooth and eat. Most of the time these are very thick and can be eaten with a spoon just like ice cream. If it is a bit too sour for your taste simply add in a tablespoon of honey to sweeten it.

**Apple Pie Oatmeal**

Some people may consider this a breakfast, but personally if something tastes like apple pie I prefer to use it as a desert.

You will need:

- ½ a cup of steel cut oats
- 2 cups of water
- 1 cup of chopped apples- about 1 apple
- ½ teaspoon ground cinnamon
- ¼ teaspoon allspice

- Honey

Combine all of the ingredients in a small sauce pan and bring to a boil. Reduce the heat and allow to simmer until it is fully cooked. If you would like the flavor to be stronger, you can double all of the spices and the honey will be drizzled on top of the finished oatmeal.

# Chapter 6: Clean Eating Tips

Finally, I want to give you a few tips that will help you be successful when it comes to clean eating. There are going to be times when it is hard for you to go against the mainstream when it comes to what you are eating but you need to remember that today there are thousands of people who are taking part in this lifestyle change and that you are not alone.

1. Remember that this is not a diet, but a lifestyle change. You should never feel as if you are deprived when you are eating clean. You should always eat your fill and never leave the table hungry. This type of eating needs to continue for the rest of your life. If you stop eating this way you will go back to being fat, you will go back to being sick and you will go back to being unhappy.

2. When you are eating real food you don't have to worry about counting calories or worrying about over eating. You are going to become fuller quicker because you are eating healthy foods that your body is made to eat.

3. Exercise is going to help you lose weight faster, but it is not the way to lose weight and keep it off. Although getting enough exercise is important to your overall health it is not focused on in clean eating. With that being said I do feel that it is important for you to make sure you are getting exercise on a daily basis. This does not have to be strenuous exercise simply something that you enjoy such as going for a walk or working in your garden.

4. When people decide to change their life and eat clean I always suggest that if it is possible they create their own garden. Not only will this provide you with an abundance of healthy food it will give you a sense of accomplishment as well. Studies have shown that those who grow gardens reduce their risk of depression and eat healthier than those who do not.

5. Do not become discouraged if you fail. We all fail at one point of another. A fizzy drink, candy bar or chips begins to call our name and we simply give in. That is okay, it is going to happen as long as it is not on a regular basis it is okay. Simply pick yourself up again and get back on the clean eating band wagon. One slip is not going to kill you or cause you to not lose weight.

6. Water is of utmost importance. I cannot stress enough how important water is to for your health. If you are dehydrated you have a higher chance of overeating, you have a higher chance of getting sick and a higher chance of obesity. Remember, 70 percent of your body is made up of water and if you are dehydrated, your body is not going to function properly.

7. Don't just eat the meals that I have given you in this book. One of the great things about clean eating is that you get to discover food again. You get to learn how to cook real food that is colorful and flavorful. Don't just stick to what I have given you, but after the first 21 days explore more clean eating recipes, try coming up with your own. Look at foods that you enjoy and try to find a way to make them so that they fit into your clean eating lifestyle.

8. Don't let anyone tell you that you are doing it wrong. I will be honest with you, when I first started doing this I had so many people tell me that I was crazy, that I had no idea what I was doing and that it was not the way to get healthy. Then I took a good look at who this information was coming from. These were people who were overweight, sick and looked like zombies. When people begin giving you unwanted advice please look at where the advice is coming from and don't get discouraged.

Clean eating is a way for you to change your life right now. It does not matter how old you are or how sick you are. With clean eating you can turn your health around, you can lose weight, have more energy and begin to look beautiful once again. Clean eating reduces aging, helps to heal the body from the inside out and even boosts productivity in one's life. Take the next 21 days and see how it can change your life.

# Conclusion

Making the choice to start eating healthier is one of the best decisions you can make. Not only will eating a clean diet make you feel better by gaining energy and look better by losing weight, but it will also make you live longer. Too many people take their diet for granted. They abuse it, and in the end they pay the consequences. It might take a little more effort to cook your meals and eat less processed food, but trust me it's worth it in the end.

I hope this book will enable you to make healthier choices that will ultimately lead to a happier and healthier life

Thank you again for buying this book!

Cathy Harwell

# Related Reading

I have the perfect complement to this book on the clean eating diet to further help you with your fitness and weight loss goals. In order to take advantage of your diet and get the quickest results you need to fully understand how your physical fitness can have a huge impact. Calisthenics and body weight exercises are some of the easiest and most efficient ways to workout.

I highly recommend you check out the book, '***30 Minutes to Ripped – Get Your Dream Body Fast with Body Weight Exercises and Calisthenics***'. It is available on Amazon in print and digital format.

Cathy Harwell

Scan Above Image or Go To -
https://www.amazon.com/dp/B015158ZIW/

*Clean Eating*

# Stop... Before you close this book get your free bonus...

Scan Above to Claim Bonus

Or Go To: http://bit.ly/1NKyFuQ

**101 Life Success Tips – Start Accomplishing Your Goals Today!**
Steve Williams is a motivational expert that has helped thousands of people accomplish their dreams and goals. Here are a few tips that he has learned along the way to improving success in his life quickly.

---------------------------------

1. **Use Visualization.** Visualize what your life will be like when you accomplish your goals. If you cannot see yourself accomplishing your goals than chances are that you will not accomplish them. Remember that you are to keep your eye on the prize at the end of the road. There will be times when you feel as if you are stuck and that you are not making any progress toward your goal, but what you need to do when this happens is to remember what your life

will be like in 6 months or a year if you continue to work toward your goals. Spend a few minutes with your eyes closed visualizing how great you will feel and all of the changes that will take place in your life once you reach these goals.

2. **Read Books, a Lot of Books**. For each of these tips there is a book out there that will give you deeper insight into each tip. Spend time reading each and every day. This will not only exercise your brain as well as help you learn, but it will help to relieve the stress that you have to deal with on a day to day basis. Even if you are not reading a book about self-improvement make sure you take some time each day to read. Reading fiction books helps to release the creativity we have within ourselves, which can help you solve problems down the road.

3. **Accept That You Are Responsible for Your Life.** You are in charge of your life and no one else. You cannot blame your failures on your parents or on what happened to you when you were in high school. You need to work through any issues that you may have but while doing so understand that no one makes your life what it is except you. If you are not succeeding in life, no one has caused this except for you and when you are successful you will have no one to thank for it except yourself.

4. **Learn How to Accept Failure and LEARN from it**. Failure, it is something that all of us will face at one point in our lives no matter what we do to avoid it. You have two choices when it comes to failure, you can either allow the failure to upset you and stop you in your tracks or you can learn from the failure and change what you do in the future. One example of this may be that you are trying to lose weight, you are tempted by a chocolate cake

and end up eating all of it. Now you have failed, you can either choose to give up on your weight loss goals and eat lots of chocolate cake in the following days, which will most likely cause you to gain more weight or you can learn from your mistake, understand that you lack the will power to stop eating after a small piece of chocolate cake, avoid it in the future and move on with your diet and weight loss plan.

5. **Do the Things That You Dread the Most First.** No matter what it is that you want to do, you should always do the things that you dread the most first, this is called eating the frog. This way you are not putting these tasks off while finishing up more enjoyable tasks, you simply do them, get them out of the way and then you can move on to the tasks that you will enjoy more.

This is a brand new report that will show you 101 quick ways to improve your life success. These are just a sample. You can have the entire report <u>for free here.</u>

Cathy Harwell

# Check Out My Other Books

Below, you'll find some of my other popular books on Amazon and Kindle. Simply scan the link below to visit my author page on Amazon to see my works.

**Direct Link -** http://www.amazon.com/Cathy-Harwell/e/B0125AD4G4/

**Clean Eating – Fire Up Your Weight Loss and Energy With Delicious Clean Eating Recipes**

**Ketogenic Diet – Amazing 30 Day Weight Loss Plan Start Your Anti-Inflammatory Diet Today!**

**30 Minutes To Ripped – Get Your Dream Body Fast With Body Weight Exercises And Calisthenics**

If the links do not work, for whatever reason, you can simply search for these titles on the Amazon website to find them.

Made in the USA
Middletown, DE
14 May 2017